D1710644

F-117A NIGHTHAWKS

★ ★ ★

BY DEREK ZOBEL

BELLWETHER MEDIA · MINNEAPOLIS, MN

Are you ready to take it to the extreme?
Torque books thrust you into the action-packed
world of sports, vehicles, and adventure. These books
may include dirt, smoke, fire, and dangerous stunts.
WARNING: read at your own risk.

Library of Congress Cataloging-in-Publication Data

Zobel, Derek, 1983-
  F-117A Nighthawks / by Derek Zobel.
      p. cm. − (Torque: military machines)
  Includes bibliographical references and index.
  Summary: "Amazing photography and engaging information explain the technologies and
capabilities of the F-117A Nighthawks. Intended for students in grades 3 through 7"−Provided by
publisher.
  ISBN-13: 978-1-60014-221-5 (hardcover : alk. paper)
  ISBN-10: 1-60014-221-4 (hardcover : alk. paper)
 1. F-117 (Jet fighter plane)−Juvenile literature. I. Title.

  UG1242.F5Z619 2008
  623.74'63−dc22   2008019866

This edition first published in 2009 by Bellwether Media.

The photographs in this book are reproduced through the courtesy of the United States Department of
Defense.

Printed in the United States of America.

CONTENTS

THE F-117A NIGHTHAWK
IN ACTION

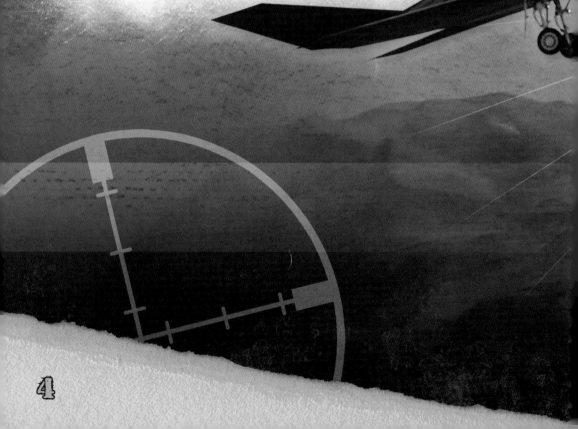

Deep in enemy territory, a dangerous new weapon has been developed. The United States Air Force must secretly destroy the factory where it is being built.

An F-117A Nighthawk takes off from a U.S. Air Force base. It cruises toward the target.

As the F-117A nears the target, it opens its **bomb bay** and drops a **laser-guided bomb (LGB)**. The bomb locks onto the enemy factory and blasts into it. The factory is destroyed. The F-117A turns around and returns to its base.

STEALTH GROUND-ATTACK AIRCRAFT

The F-117A was the U.S. Air Force's first **stealth** ground-attack aircraft. Its first flight was in 1981, but it first saw action in 1989. The F-117A's stealth technology was important to military operations until it was retired from service in 2007.

★ **FAST FACT** ★

The F-117A Nighthawk was replaced by the F-22 Raptor.

The F-117A was designed to fly into
enemy territory, drop bombs, and return
to base. Pilots could do these **missions** and
stay hidden from the enemy. This was a
big advantage to the U.S. Air Force.

WEAPONS AND FEATURES

The F-117A carried all kinds of bombs. One kind was the laser-guided bomb. Standard bombs simply fall toward the ground when dropped. Laser-guided bombs are guided toward their target by computers.

REMOVE BEFORE FLIGHT

MJ-1B

The F-117A's speed also helped it complete missions quickly. Its top speed was 617 miles (993 kilometers) per hour.

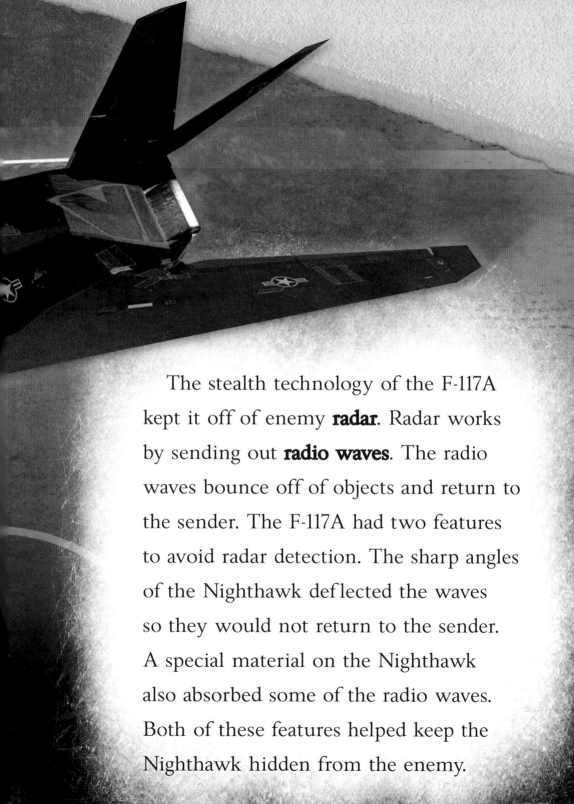

The stealth technology of the F-117A kept it off of enemy **radar**. Radar works by sending out **radio waves**. The radio waves bounce off of objects and return to the sender. The F-117A had two features to avoid radar detection. The sharp angles of the Nighthawk deflected the waves so they would not return to the sender. A special material on the Nighthawk also absorbed some of the radio waves. Both of these features helped keep the Nighthawk hidden from the enemy.

F-117A NIGHTHAWK SPECIFICATIONS:

Primary Function: Stealth ground-attack aircraft

Length: 69 feet, 9 inches (20.08 meters)

Height: 12 feet, 9.5 inches (3.78 meters)

Weight: 29,500 pounds (13,380 kilograms)

Wingspan: 43 feet, 4 inches (13.2 meters)

Speed: 617 miles (993 kilometers) per hour

Range: 1,070 miles (1,720 kilometers)

F-117A MISSIONS

F-117A missions were usually performed at night. The plane's black color helped keep it from being seen by the naked eye. Once an F-117A was in the air, computers could control the mission. The computers tracked the location of the target and the location of the F-117A, then calculated when to open the bomb bay and drop its bombs.

The F-117A used a drag parachute during landing to help slow it down.

However, powerful computers weren't enough for a successful mission. A single pilot flew each F-117A. Nighthawks were difficult to fly because of their awkward shape. The most skilled pilots were needed to fly them. Stealth technology helped protect them on their missions, but flying a plane in enemy territory is always dangerous.

GLOSSARY

bomb bay—the compartment of an aircraft from which bombs are dropped

laser-guided bomb (LGB)—an explosive that locks onto a target marked with a laser

mission—a military task

radar—a sensor system that uses radio waves to locate objects

radio waves—waves sent out by radar to detect objects

stealth—hidden

TO LEARN MORE

AT THE LIBRARY

Green, Michael and Gladys. *Stealth Attack Fighters: The F-117A Nighthawks*. Minneapolis, Minn.: Capstone, 2008.

Stone, Lynn M. *Nighthawk F-117A*. Vero Beach, Fla.: Rourke, 2004.

Zobel, Derek. *United States Air Force*. Minneapolis, Minn.: Bellwether, 2008.

ON THE WEB

Learning more about military machines is as easy as 1, 2, 3.

1. Go to www.factsurfer.com

2. Enter "military machines" into search box.

3. Click the "Surf" button and you will see a list of related web sites.

With factsurfer.com, finding more information is just a click away.

INDEX